IELTS speaking test

Happy to present new course on preparation for IELTS speaking test. The course is based on 300+ recent speaking questions asked in IELTS tests; we have collected these questions from our students who appeared for IELTS test in different parts of the world.

The suggested answers are created by a group of experienced trainers, some of whom have recently appeared for IELTS test themselves and successfully cleared the test.

We are also presenting practice questions along with questions that have been answered.

IELTS Speaking test is Conducted in three sections

1. Personal section
2. Que Card Section
3. Follow up questions or general questions

Description

1. Personal Section, you get 4 to 5 questions related to topics about you, examples could be Your Job, Your school, family, hometown etc.

2. Que Card, you get one question which has some add on questions related to the same topic. You get one minute to think or make small notes and you are required to speak for up to 2 minutes.

3. General questions or follow up questions, these questions could be follow up questions from que card questions or all together different question about common social matters.

How are you scored?

You are scored in four areas

a. **Grammar**
b. **Diversified Vocabulary**
c. **Pronunciation**
d. **Task Completion**

How to answer the questions:

The most important thing to keep in mind while answering questions is, it's a conversation and not a question answer session.

Do not answer the questions like a quiz

Try to give an opening sentence to your answer followed by main body or addressing the task given in the question and a concluding statement.

Suggested time to answer the questions

a. Personal section: You should speak about 30 to 40 seconds on each question
b. Que Card: Speak for up to 2 minutes on que card question, you must address all sub questions
c. Follow Up Questions: You should speak up to 40 seconds on these questions

Shopping:

1. Where do people in your country buy grocery?

In smaller towns normally people buy food items from neighborhood grocery store, while in metro cities they prefer departmental store and the latest trend is online grocery stores especially in large cities where people prefer to save time and avoid hassle of driving and parking.

2. Is it better to buy clothes in small shops?

It depends on the clothes that one is purchasing, if I am purchasing my office wear or any cloth for special occasions, I would prefer to buy it from a branded store, however if I am buying T Shirts or a casual wear cloth, I would prefer to buy it in small shop, they may offer a variety of choices at reasonable rates.

3. What are the advantages of Internet shopping?

Off late internet shopping is gaining popularity in my country, there are many advantages that internet shopping offers, one can see multiple products from multiple vendors and go through product descriptions, get to know the lowest offer on the product all by just using a click. It saves time and driving expenses and is without the hassle of going to multiple stores to see all variants of the product.

4. What is good customer service?

A good customer service is what we all expect when we are customers, whether we are purchasing a small item or a large industrial supply. In my opinion a good customer service is being truthful and respectful to the customer and addressing their needs. Showing respect to customer giving correct information about the product or services being offered understanding the customer's requirement and suggesting the best product followed by a good after sales service.

5. Why do some shops provide better customer service than other shops?

I would think this is a clear reflection of thought process of management of the shop, some shops believe in long term business, they ensure that they take care of customer's needs and suggest the best deal along with after sales service, it may reduce the profit margin temporarily however they win customers for ever. While some businesses would be too focused on today's sales figures or profits and choose not to give best customer service.

6. Why is shopping such a popular activity?

Shopping is very popular in almost all age groups, it takes away the stress or any other negative thoughts that the person may be going through, The excitement of looking at multiple product getting to know its features, looking at vibrant color of clothes, using imagination to see its usage makes us happy and gives a sense of satisfaction. It can also take one away from a monotonous life.

7. What are the advantages to society of a highly developed shopping centre?

A highly developed shopping center is gaining popularity in almost all parts of the country, It gives the buyers an opportunity to look at multiple stores for their purchase needs while being at one destination only that is it saves time and driving hassles, it also gives the buyer a chance to look at multiple stores for the similar products. One can shop for products ranging from groceries to electronics to clothing and may also offer dining and other entertainment facilities. It offers a sense of competition among businesses so that customer can get most reasonable deal.

8. Is our society becoming increasingly materialistic?

Yes I would agree that the society is becoming materialistic, we have started valuing the physical assets or attributes more than relations, emotions or knowledge. Our preferences have moved from leading a life with satisfaction to working towards acquiring more. This is also causing a lot of stress among all of us, as needs can be fulfilled but it's difficult to fulfill wants.

9. What kind of things do you prefer shopping for?

For me Shopping is a work that must be completed quickly, my choices in shopping are simple, jeans, trousers, t shirts, what I enjoy most while shopping is purchasing Electronics, watches, shoes.

I prefer shopping for clothes, Watches, shoes, electronics, and any other accessories. Since the fashion is ever changing I enjoy shopping as per the prevailing trends. I do prefer window shopping when budget is limited.

10. In what kind of places do you like to go shopping?

My personal choice for shopping is a neat and clean market place, preferably less crowded. I prefer to shop at malls for clothing and electronics, however if I have to purchase casual wear or some small items I like to visit stand alone shops.

11. What effect has online shopping had in your country?

Online shopping is gaining popularity in my country in recent times, It has created a great competition to traditional brick and mortar stores as the consumer can check different websites and get to know the lowest deal for the same product. It ensures that the stores have to offer the best discount possible to consumer to remain competitive, it saves time and fuel bills for consumer its hassle free no need to drive and park, reduces pollution, creates additional employment in logistics industry. Overall I would say it has made a significant impact.

12. What would you recommend that tourists buy from your country?

When tourists visit my country they actually help all sections of our economy like tourism, hotels, small vendors etc. My recommendation to tourists would be to buy handicrafts, colorful dresses, artificial jewellery and designer furniture.

13.   Do you ever shop at a street market?

Yes I do shop at street market; normally I would buy smaller items from street market, Fresh vegetables, Fruits, smaller plastic items for household usage, sometimes I buy a toy for my children from a neighborhood street market.

14.   Have you ever been to a night market? What was special about it?

Yes I have been to Night Market in my city many a times, it was a wonderful experience to be at a street or night market as you may call it, there were lots of food vendors who were selling their freshly prepared delicacies at very reasonable rates. Different types of cuisines available at one place also there was a lot of jewellery and some useful household items that were being sold. The best part was this market was in a street that is usually a business area during day time that is it was creating additional employment for a large number of people.

15.   Do you think there will be more street markets in your city in future or fewer?

Although many would believe that departmental stores will replace street markets, my opinion is absolutely different, I believe as the city population keeps growing the demand for fresh vegetables, freshly cooked street side meals at reasonable rates will keep increasing, furthermore there are a lot of small household items that people will continue to buy from street markets, I believe the number of street markets will keep increasing in future.

Prcatice Questions

16. Why do you think some people use internet for shopping?

   I suggest use reasons like... Convenience of shopping at odd hours, no hassle of driving and parking, saves time, easy return policy, price comparison, discounted deals etc.

17. What kinds of things are easy to buy and sell online? Can you share some examples?
18. Do you think shopping on the internet will be more popular in future? Why?
19. How important are clothes and fashion to you?
20. What kind of clothes do you like to wear? Why?

   I suggest you answer as per your individual likings, you may say, I like Jeans and T shirts/tops as it is easier to carry and maintain.

21. Do you think the clothes we wear say about our personality?

22. How do you feel about shopping for clothes?

23. Would you prefer to have a lot of clothes or only a few, better quality ones?

Movies:

24. When was the last time you went to the cinema?

I went to the cinema only last week on Sunday, I had few friends visiting me in the afternoon and we decided to watch a movie together, we quickly booked ticket online went to a nearby cinema and watched a movie, it was after a long time when we were watching a movie together and it was a wonderful time to be with friends cracking jokes and watching movie.

25. How popular are cinemas where you live?

I would say cinemas are very popular and a major source of entertainment for people where I live, one can notice a large crowd in most of the cinema theatres always, People watch movies as per their choice of actors and themes some may like family oriented drama or comedy movies while some prefer action or romantic movies. Overall cinemas area big crowd puller.

26.   What sort of films you enjoy the most?

I enjoy watching comedy movies as it gives me a reason to laugh and smile, I find comedy movies as a good stress buster, they take me away from my usual routine of work or any other thoughts that may give me stress, I always feel relaxed after watching a comedy movie.

27.   Where do you prefer to watch films, at the cinema or at home?

Although I do watch films at home however my preference is always to watch films at the cinema as the Dolby digital sound system and big screen makes the entire experience much better, sometimes if it is a three dimensional film the effect gets much better if I watch it in Cinema.

28.   Why do people still enjoy going to the cinema to watch a film?

People go to watch a film for entertainment purpose and the entertainment value for the same film goes up with the help of better sound system, large screen etc. the complete atmosphere of cinema theatre makes one get more engrossed in the film and makes it more enjoyable, most of the time people prefer to have some snacks along with film, someone else serving you snacks while you enjoy the film is one more reason for many to go to cinema.

29.   What sort of influence can films have on people?

Films have both audio and visual effect and many a times can create a great influence on people simply by the way the director or narrator wants to present a storyline, be it getting a positive thought or feeling of being romantic, films worldwide have been able to create a great deal of influence on people.

30.   Should filmmakers be responsible for the impact their films can have on people?

I would not say responsible, however I must agree that film makers must be sensitive to the fact that their films can have long lasting impact on people who watch their films, sometimes too much violence could be disturbing for some audience, or glorifying a bad character could mislead youngsters, in my opinion the filmmaker should always try to present a positive side of good characters.

31.   Are film stars paid too much money, in your opinion?

It is true that film stars make a lot of money through films, commercials and stage appearances, but we have to look at the career of film stars as well, acting as a career is extremely risky, fist of all its very difficult to be a successful film start, secondly failure of one or two films can make a film star lose a lot of work, there are many stories of success as well as failure of film stars, Lastly Films are a business and commercials are purely for promotions and generating more revenue and that is the reason film stars are paid high as per their market value.

Practice Questions

32. Do you think there is too much violence in modem movies?
33. What do you think about film censorship? Is it necessary?
34. What was the last film you saw? Did you enjoy it?
35. Tell me about your favorite actor.
36. Do you think popularity of cinema has increased in recent years?
37. Do you prefer to watch films on real life heroes?
38. Should films and television be censored or should we be free to choose what we see?
39. Is film a useful medium to create awareness?
40. What sort of things do you believe should be censored in films?
41. What types of movie is more popular among the youth?
42. Do you prefer watching films in the cinema or at home?

Theatre:

43. Why do some people prefer to go to theatre than to the cinema?

Theaters are not as popular as cinema, however some people prefer to go to theatre as they believe films are not real, they have been edited, corrected and the actors are not acting it is a lot to do with computer graphics, while in theatre they get to see live acting with real actors and real acting. They prefer to watch a real play live as against a recorded and edited film.

44. How often do you go to theatre?

To be honest I am not much a theatre fan, I have not been to a live theatre in years, last time I went to theatre is when one of my friends was part of a theater group and encouraged me to watch theater and I did like the play however it was more to do with the fact that I knew someone who was in the theatre group.

45. What would be the thrills and challenges of being a theatre director?

In my opinion it is an extremely challenging job to be a theatre director, you do not have any control once the artist goes live on the stage, there is no way one can edit or redo the same scene, furthermore if one artist falls sick finding a replacement is extremely difficult in a short span of time.

Career:

46. Who gives advice about career in your country?

In my country career advice is generally given by parents and teachers, Parents understand the needs of their children their skills, likings and disliking and their ability, also if there is a teacher that knows the child's strengths and weaknesses they are in a better position to give advice about career. Some people also prefer to take help of a professional career counselor.

47. **Do you think it is better to choose a career on one's own or to take advice from others about the choice?**

I would think this entirely depends on the thought process of individual, some individuals are very clear about their choices, strengths and weaknesses, however some may not be equally sure, we must keep in mind that many people make a change in their choice of career once they get into it, so keeping in mind both the views I think one should listen to others advice however may make decision depending on what they think is the best for them.

48. **Tell me about a good piece of advice someone gave you.**

While I was about to start my career after college, I was in two minds whether to continue with education for Masters or start working, I spoke to my dad, he gave me a patient hearing and asked all the pros and cons of continuing for masters degree, then suggested I must go for Masters as jobs will always be available and with a masters degree I will have chances of getting a better job. Till date I value this as a great advise that was given to me.

49. **How do you feel when someone gives you advice against your choice?**

It happens many a times that someone shares their thought and advices one against their choice and it may not sound good at all, however with past experiences I have learnt that any advice that is against your choice is worth a second thought, I may disagree with the advice but I make it a point to critically think what the other person is suggesting.

Practice Questions

50. Can you tell me about your current job?

    Speak about the job that you currently doing, mention you Industry like hospital, software, mention your position, a brief description of your job.

51. What do you like or dislike about your current job?
52. What plans do you have for your career in future?
53. Do you think knowledge of computers is important in your chosen career?
54. Do you plan to learn new skills in future?
55. Have you ever given up anything you used to do in free time?
56. Tell me about some hobbies would you like to practice in future?
57. Do you share similar interests with your friends or family members?

Festivals:

58.   What are the most important festivals in your culture?

There are many festivals in our culture, some of the most important festivals are Deepawali, Dussehra, Holi, GiruParv. Like any other community we celebrate festivals with our friends and family, prepare delicious food, perform aarti and pooja at home or temples.

59.   How do people celebrate New Year in your culture?

There is a general sense of excitement all around the community as the New Year comes, people tend to make plans for New Year, the youngsters celebrate New Year by getting in to parties in their groups, while families celebrate by organizing parties together at homes or banquet halls. Some exchange gifts and presents and some people treat their families and friends with great food.

60. **Which festival did you enjoy celebrating most when you were a child?**

As a child I would always be happy celebrating New year as we would get winter vacations in school for almost ten days, we would get presents on Christmas and new year, further more new Year would mean a family outing or picnic at a scenic location, I really loved the entire holidays and excitement around the new year.

61. **Which festival in another country would you like to go to?**

I would love to go to Canada to celebrate Christmas, This time around Canada is almost covered in white snow and gives a very beautiful and pleasant look; I would love to celebrate Christmas in Toronto to see the bright side of city life, great food from all multi cuisine restaurants along with chilly cold weather with snow capped countryside.

62. **Are family occasions as important today as they were for earlier generations?**

Ideally speaking yes family occasions are as important today as they were earlier, however with changing times the occasions have become shorter and are mostly planned over weekends or keeping holidays in mind. Earlier weddings would mean the entire extended family or friends being together for days, now families live far apart and visit only for the wedding, in some cases reaching and leaving the same day.

Practice Questions

63. Why do you think festivals are important for a society?

You can say breaks monotony in life, gives reason to celebrate, festivals are mostly related to some religious activities, gives a chance to get together with family and friends. Helps us rejuvenate.

64. Would you agree that the original significance of the festivals is often lost today?

65. What roles does media play in festivals?

66. What gifts do you generally give to your family members in festivals?

67. Do you think cultural celebrations and festivals have changed in your country?

68. Is it important for the immigrants to adopt customs and festivals that are celebrated in their new country?

69. What type of special occasions are generally celebrated in your culture?

70. Is it important for families to celebrate occasions together?

71. What events in a person's life are most celebrated in your country?

72. Most families gather together on special occasions like wedding what effect does this have on family relationship?

Music:

73.   How often do you listen to music? Why?

I am not very choosy with my music, I normally listen to music while I am driving and my preference is any music which has high beats and keep me energized, sometimes when I am alone I prefer to listen to old melodious songs that helps me relax.

74.   Do you prefer to buy CDs or download music from the internet? Why?

I always prefer to buy CDs although I am aware that a lot of music can be downloaded these days; however I find it more convenient to walk into a neighborhood store and pick music of one of my favorite artist. Since I do not listen to a lot of music buying a CD does not hurt my pocket much.

75.   Have you always liked the same kind of music? Why? Why not?

No I would say my choice of music has changed with age, while I was a teenager, I would listen to latest songs from films and as I went to college I started listening to rock music more, these days my choice of music is limited to melodies from old movies and any music that plays on radio while I drive. I think change in choice of music can be attributed to age and preferences.

76.   Is there a musical instrument you would like to learn to play? Why? Why not?

Given a choice I would love to learn how to play Guitar, I have watched a lot of artists perform live using guitar and somehow it gives me excitement as to how they can create such impactful music with just one musical instrument.

77.   Have you ever played a musical instrument?

While in college I tried playing Guitar, one of my friends was very good at playing different musical instruments, he gave me few lessons on how to play guitar and I was excited as I learnt the basics of Guitar.

78.   Do you think some people are naturally good at music?

I am not very good at music and do not have a great understanding of music, However I have come across few people who are really good at understanding the music, although I know they have not taken any course in music, this makes me believe some people are naturally good at music and have a great sense of understanding music.

79.   Do you think the music industry these days is less about music and more about style?

I would disagree with the statement, in my opinion, music industry is a lot about style, appearance etc. however the soul of this industry is still music, what gets popular is music, style may be one of the components however the industry is still working on creating better music.

Family:

80. Could you tell me about your family?

I leave it to students to give a brief description about their family.

81. How often do you have visitors to your home? What do you do?

Since life is too hectic for almost every one that I know, we do not have a lot of visitors, sometimes we invite our friends and families for a lunch or dinner, we prepare food for them and some of them get few items that they want to share with all, we enjoy the day with lots of food, talking to each other cracking jokes, children playing around and relax.

82. How do you feel about staying the night at the homes of friends or relatives?

When we go for functions that last over few days we stay with friends and relatives, it could be for wedding or some kind of festival that runs through few days, it's kind of a holiday and I enjoy being relaxed talking to friends getting involved in any group work that needs to be completed.
I love to keep talking to my friends and their family members before going to bed.

83. How has visiting others changed in your country in last ten years?

I would say visiting others has become a planned activity now as compared to ten years back when it was more to simply meet and relax, everyone that I know is too occupied with their routine life and rarely get chance to visit family or friends, earlier people would visit their relatives and spend quality time with them, These days visits by friends and relatives has become more planned activity with fixed date and time of arrival and departure, some people carry small business activity along with visiting family.

84.   Tell me about the accommodation you are currently living in?

I would suggest my students to describe their current accommodation as they see it.

85.   Do you think you will stay where you are living for a while?

I have been living in the same area for a long time; I am so used to of living in my current neighborhood and have developed a level of comfort around with neighbors, stores, restaurants, friends etc. My children go to school in the same area even their friends live in this neighborhood, so I think I will continue to live in my current location for a while.

Practice Questions

86. Who do you live with?

87. Do you spend much time with your family?

88. What do you do when you are all together?

89. Do you have a large or small family?

90. What sort of things do you do with your family members?

91. Do you get on well with your family members?

Writing:

92. What different types of writing do you do for example letters emails, reports or fiction?

The kind of job that I am in I mostly write emails and reports, I am required to write reports on the developments made by my team in terms of the project that is assigned to us, this report is to be share with the management every week, also as per the nature of my work I have to respond to e mails that I receive at work and seek clarification from others at work.

93. Do you prefer writing with a pen or using a computer? Why?

Since I started working all writing activities for me are done using computer and that has become a habit, so to be honest I have lost my habits of writing using a pen and I prefer writing using computer.

94. Do you write more now or less than you did a few years ago? Why?

When I was in college I would write a lot, whether its assignments or self study or noting down important texts from a book, I would do a lot of writing activity, since I started working my writings have shortened and its limited to e mails wherein the emphasis is on keeping it short crisp and precise, so I would say I write less now as compared to few years ago.

95. Do you like to write stories or poems? Why? Why not?

No I do not like to write stories or poems, I would do some fiction or story writing while I was in school, however with time the habit of writing stories has changed into writing on subject matter or writing reports at work.

Food:

96.   What is your favorite Meal?

My favorite meal is home cooked chicken and rice, sometimes I cook for myself over the weekend or if it's a holiday, for me it's a total experience, I enjoy every bit of it whether its cooking or enjoying a spicy chicken with simple rice.

97.   Do you prefer to eat out or eat at home?

I always prefer to eat at home, as I do not like to eat very spicy or thick gravy food; a home cooked simple meal is what I want after a hard day's work. Eating out occasionally is good as I can satisfy by taste buds trying a different cuisine however my choice is always a home cooked meal.

98.   Are there any traditional meals that you would like to recommend? Why?

Traditionally Indians have preferred to eat spicy kidney beans cooked in gravy with rice and I may recommend the same to my friends, it's a rich and wholesome food, very high on protein and less on carbohydrates cooked with a very low amount of fat.

99.   How have peoples eating habits changed in your country?

With time a lot of habits have changed for people in almost all parts of society including eating habits, earlier people would have a lot of time available and life was not very hectic, that would mean a proper breakfast at home, home cooked lunch and a relaxed dinner, since most of us have long working hours, breakfast is generally consumed in a hurry or sometimes on the run, even lunches are mostly outside food served by workplace cafeteria. Weekend eating has almost become a part of life.

100.   Do you think people eat healthier food than they did in the past?

In recent times there is a lot of awareness that has been created towards eating healthy food, earlier most of the people would eat what they wants however with widespread coverage on food habits and calorie count on most food items people are increasingly getting conscious of their dining habits and consumer much healthier food as compared to earlier times.

101. Do you think that food prepared at home is always better than in restaurants?

It may not be necessarily correct, food prepared at home is healthy, hygienic and simple with good nutrient value, however food cooked in restaurant is meant to be sold to customers, so the restaurant food most of the times has an eye appeal, aroma and is made delicious. If I have to share my opinion I would say home cooked food is good however may not always be better than in restaurant.

102. Which are more popular in your country fast food restaurants or traditional restaurants?

In my opinion people prefer fast food restaurants over traditional restaurants, in today's life everyone is occupied and has less time available, purchasing food becomes a necessity and this is the reason people like to visit fast food restaurants to get their order quickly and have a quick meal as against sitting down ordering the food and waiting for food to be served.

103. Why do people go to restaurants when they want to celebrate important occasions?

Going to restaurants is very common in people whenever they want to celebrate an important occasion with their friends and family, it serves many purposes, they get to spend quality time together, enjoy meal to suit their taste buds, there is no hassle of cooking for a large group and it allows everyone to focus more on occasion rather than being occupied with preparation and arranging things.

104. What effects has modern technology had on the food we eat?

I would say technological advancements have made a lot of things easier and faster for all of us including our food and dining habits, like a microwave helps us get a quick meal in a matter of minutes, saves time and energy; frozen foods are gaining popularity all around, better quality refrigerators ensure we can stock and consume food for longer duration. Now we get smaller versions of Ovens that make baking food easier and faster.

105. How important do you think it is for families to eat meals together?

Although it's difficult for the entire family to be together for a dinner every day, however eating a meal together with the family is definitely a great family exercise that should be followed. Having a meal with the family can be good to connect with each other, talk about any issues that anyone is facing be it at work or school, just talk about how the day went any special plans for weekend, I would say overall it opens a healthy communication among family members.

Practice Questions

106. Tell me about your favorite food?

107. Do you prefer eating at home or in a restaurant? Why?

108. Do you prefer to eat in a fine dining restaurant or a fast food outlet?

109. Tell me about a special delicacy from your country.

110. What kind of food do you enjoy?

111. Do you like to spend much time shopping for food?

112. How often do you eat out?

113. Do you think people should take care of their diet?

114. Who prepares the meals you eat?

115. How often do you cook for self or family?

116. Do you like cooking?

117. What do you think makes cooking easy?

118. Do you think cooking is a difficult job?

119. Do you think kitchen equipment, such as a dishwasher or food processor are a good help in modern day kitchens?

120. Is there a favorite restaurant of yours where you normally eat? Why?

121. In what ways are people's dining habits changing these days?

122. Do you like to try out a new cuisine?

Your Country:

123. Do most people live in houses or apartments in your country?

In my country most of the people live in houses, Although living in apartments is fast catching up in larger cities due to lack of space, security concerns and lack of time to maintain area around ones house, however in countryside or small towns people still prefer to live in independent houses.

124. What do people usually do in free time in your country?

Usually people like to connect with their family and friends in their free time, if they have time they would like to visit their family or friends, if they don't have that much time, they may want to connect over the phone or social media, some people also prefer to watch TV soaps, sports or watch movies.

125.   What do you enjoy most about living in your country?

I was born and raised in this country, have my family and lots of friends and relatives here, what I enjoy is catching up with some of them every now and then, I like the fact that my country is growing at a rapid pace lots of employment opportunities are coming up, I also enjoy the availability of food outlets offering different cuisines at reasonable rates.

126.   Would you say that your country is a good place to visit? Why?

Yes I would always say that my country is a good place to visit, it's a peaceful nation which is not very costly for someone to visit, there are a lot of tourist attractions available in almost all parts of country and also the country is fast becoming a business hub for business personnel to travel and explore business possibilities.

Advertising:

127.   How do you feel about the amount of advertising on television?

Sometimes it does seem that there are too many advertisements on television, however we must keep in mind in order to provide quality entertainment programs to viewers the television needs to have revenue, since the television programs are mostly free to air or come at a very low rate to consumer the television company is dependent upon advertisements to generate revenue, I personally feel television companies are showing only the right amount of advertisements.

128.   In what ways has television advertising changed in last ten years?

The world is changing rapidly and with the changing world the choice of consumer is changing as well, for example a phone with video calling features was unheard of in most parts of the world and impact of social media was very limited ten years back, however in today's world everyone is on social media and every phone is a smart phone, it has created a market for new and emerging businesses also there is a large population of youth who would be more willing to try a new product that is launched, all these are triggering change in the way advertisement in done The advertisers are getting innovative in the way they approach their customers, using digital technology or print/electronic advertising.

129.   To what extent are people influenced by the advertising they see on television?

Advertising on television has both audio and visual effect and it does make an impact on all of us, if we get to know about a product that is suited to our needs or if the product features attract us, people tend to give it a try and they may continue with the new product as they feel it is best suited to their needs. In my opinion people especially the younger generation gets influenced by the advertising they see on television.

Practice Questions

130.   Do you think advertisement on internet is good for businesses or society in general?
131.   How do you think the internet will affect shopping patterns in the fixture?
132.   What effect has the internet had on the way people communicate with each other?
133.   Do think the Internet is being used more and more for communication?
134.   Do you think information from the internet is reliable?

Work:

135.   What job do you do?

I would leave it to the reader to explain their respective work.

136.   What skills do you need for your job?

I would encourage the reader to discuss actual skills needed for their respective jobs.

137.   What do you particularly like about your job?

Since I work as a project coordinator for my company, my job is always exciting, everyday is a new day and everyday there are new developments that I come across, also I may face a new challenge every now and then, what I like about my job is getting a new challenge and efforts that myself and my team puts to overcome the challenge. The satisfaction that I get on successful completion of the project.

(I may also suggest that the answer shared above is just a guideline, the reader is best advised to answer this question based on their work experience)

Practice Questions

138.   What are the best ways to prepare for a job interview?

139.   Which jobs do you think are the most difficult?

140.   What can employers do to keep their employees happy and motivated?

141.   Do you think there should be a specific dress code at workplace?

142.   Is it better to stay in one job for a long time to have many different jobs?

143.   If you decide to run your own business, what would it be?

144.   What things would you consider before setting up your own business?

Study:

145.   What subjects are you studying?

I leave this to my students to answer based on their current studies.

146.   Why did you want to study the subject?

I leave this to my students to answer based on their current studies.

147.   How long have you been studying (Medicine, engineering, management etc.)?

I leave this to my students to answer based on their current studies.

148.   In general what opportunities are available to students after they leave school?

After leaving schools students can go to University for higher education like bachelors and masters degrees, they may take up a vocational training course or a job oriented diploma course to enhance their skills and take up jobs as trained workforce, students may also join some organizations as apprentice trainee to get on the job training for technical skills.

149.   How do you think school life differs from college life?

In my opinion school life is free of any stress, whereas college life is about dreams and working hard towards your dreams. In school we have to only worry about our studies and rest all is taken care of by family members and even teachers are extremely helpful while at college we have to start preparing ourselves for future life, goals are set and we have to work hard to achieve goals, we become independent, managing self and managing expenses become part of life. Although the fun element in college is higher we can go to parties enjoy trips with friends.

150.   How important do you think it is for individuals to carry on learning after they have finished school and university?

We live in a world that is ever changing, something that was unique and had huge demand in market few years back is obsolete now and is replaced by a new product, for example today's generation does not even know what pager was and a Smartphone with video calling features was unheard of 10 years back, we know technology is improving every day, new theories, new scientific inventions, new developments are a part of today's world, so it is very important for all to continue learning even after finishing schools and universities, example could be a surgeon learning robotic surgery.

151. What can schools do to help students prepare for the next stage in their lives?

Schools have the responsibility to ensure they provide best possible education to their students, however they must also prepare their students for next stage in their life, it can be helping them with college admissions, sharing information with students about all the options available to them after school like, further education and names of universities, the courses they offer, career options and also provide basic practical training required for any technical and vocational courses that students may wish to take.

152. What advice would you give to someone who does not like school?

If I come across a person who does not like school, I would suggest him/her to try and continue with studies as school studies cover a wide range of subjects and help us develop as a complete person, also they may start liking one or two subjects as they pay attention to and might go ahead and complete a specialization in subject of their choice.

153. Tell me something about your secondary school.

I would recommend students to give a three or four line description of their school.

154. Which subject did you find most difficult at school? Why?

During school days I somehow struggled at history, although me teachers did work hard with me to ensure I learn the subject and get better score in tests so that it does not take away my hard work in other subjects, however memorizing dates and years and kings and names of successors was too difficult for me at that time.

155.   Do you ever need that subject now? Why? Why not?

In terms of my work I do not need history at all as I took science and later picked up management in my university, however in terms of my knowledge about my country and the world, evolvement of human civilization etc. I still believe that it was good that I studied history in school; it has helped me in coming across as a more knowledgeable person.

156.   What did you enjoy about being a school students?

Similar to what most of the students feel, I love my school days, those were the days of fun, I had nothing to be worried about, the only job that I had to do was to ensure good grades in examination and luckily I had teachers and my parents who were always available to help and guide me in every manner possible.

Practice Questions

157 . Apart from academics, what else did you enjoy at school?

158. Do you think you will stay friends with people from your school?

159. What study or training would you like to do in the future?

160.. What were your favorite subjects at school?

161. Did you learn any foreign language at school?

162. What do you like/dislike about studying?

163. Do you hope to gain any qualifications?

164. Do hope to do any further studies in the future?

165. What do you remember about your first school, when you were a child?

166. What was your favorite subject in college? Why?

167. Which is the most popular sport in your country?

168. Could you tell me why you choose to study at University?

169. What type of books do you read often?

170. Do you prefer to read a book or watch a movie on the same subject and why?

171. Are printed books essential in today's digital world?

172. Can the books we read tell us about real life?

173. How important is it for children to learn to read?

174. Do you think a time will come when people get all factual information from the Internet?

175. Do you think newspapers are a good source of information?

176. How often do you read a newspaper?

177. What can we do to encourage young people to read more?

Television:

178.   How often do you watch television?

With the kind of work schedule I have, I leave for work at 7.30 in the morning and come back around six in the evening; I like to spend an hour in gym every day, so I don't get to watch television much, I would say I watch news or some comedy show for thirty minutes a day, during my week offs, I do watch some sports channels.

179. What kinds of television programmes are most popular in your country?

The most popular programs in my country are family dramas that are women oriented and have a great fan following especially with women. Other programs that are popular are reality shows where participants display their singing, dancing or any other musical skills. News and sports are especially popular with men and younger generation.

180. Is there anything you would like to change about television in your country?

Yes, I believe television in my country has become more of a medium of entertainment and is getting extremely commercialized, I would like to add few educational channels wherein reputed teachers take video lectures and these are telecasted all over the country.

Practice Questions

181. Do you watch TV often?

182. Could you tell me about your favorite TV program?

183. What's the most popular form of advertising in your country?

184. Would you like to work for an advertising agency?

185. Do you agree that advertisements for smoking or alcoholic products should be banned?

186. What role does advertising play in the society?

187. Do you think mode of advertising will change in future?

188. Do you think that governments should use laws to protect people from misleading advertising?

Home town:

189.   What kind of place is your town/city?

Please share a brief description of your city, you may want to tell about, few things like
a. History of town
b. Population
c. Weather
d. Economy/major occupation
e. Education facilities/ major colleges, Universities
f. Transportation
g. Any place of tourist interest.

190.   What's the most interesting part of your town city?

The most interesting part of my town was city fort, It was built by the ruler of the city and it was more than hundred years old. Although the fort had lost its charm over time, however it still was a great site to visit, it was a huge fort with a lake inside it , the lake had boating facility and some gardens around, it was a great family outing place for the entire city, I remember visiting the fort with my parents as a child, we would go for boating have snacks and spend the entire day watching migratory birds.

191.   Has your town/city changed in last ten years?

Yes like most of the cities my Town has changed a lot in last ten years, earlier it was a sleepy town with slow moving traffic and a very easy lifestyle, however now I notice elevated roads, small shops have been converted to Malls, stand alone cinemas have become multiplexes, One can find huge showrooms of branded electronic and dress material. New schools and colleges have opened; I also notice a large number of companies opening their offices in town that is helping young generation in getting better employment opportunities.

192.   Would you say your town/city is a good place for young people to live?

Yes my town is a good place for young people to live, it has good educational institutions and also has a university for higher studies, in recent years a large number of multinational companies have opened their offices and that create good employment opportunities for young professionals. There is an industrial zone which is just outside the city and there are many industrial houses that have their manufacturing units in the industrial zone and this creates a large number of job opportunities for skilled and unskilled young people.

193.   Is your home town a good place to live? Why?

Yes, my hometown is a good place to live, it is not a huge city, commuting around the city is easy and public transport is available, although it's a small city but has a lot of employment facilities available. A large number of software companies and multinational companies have their offices in our town and these companies have created a lot of jobs, trading is one area which is very popular in my town and trading is the biggest source of employment. The climate of the city is good and generally cooler than most parts of the country, there are many schools and colleges and overall education system is very good.

194.   What sort of jobs do people do in your home town?

Trading and jobs related to trading are the biggest source of employment in my town, also there area large number of multinational companies that have established their offices here along with some software companies if I say these companies are another major source of employment that would be true.

195.   Where did you play in your home town when you were a child?

As a child I would play with other kids from my neighborhood in the park in our colony as we grew to be teenagers we started going to a nearby stadium to play, the stadium had a large play ground for games like soccer, cricket etc, it also had a gymnasium and few other sports facility like badminton and table tennis.

196.   In which part of your home town do most people live?

Most of the people live in the central part of the town, where there is easy availability of markets, educational institutions and railway station is nearby too. In recent years there are new and modern apartment complexes being built on the outskirts of the town and a lot of people prefer to live there due to additional feature like swimming pool, security and gated community.

197.   Are there any famous buildings in your home town?

Almost 15 years back there was a five star hotel built in our town it has a ship shaped building and has a unique architecture, being a five start hotel it is very well maintained and gives a stunning look, furthermore the blue glass on the outside of the building makes it very attractive, it is simply the most famous building of our town.

198.   In what type of buildings do most people in your home town live?

Earlier most of the people lived in independent houses, however with rapid growth of population and a large number of people coming here for employment and business

purpose there is a rapid shift in the type of houses people live in, now a large number of people prefer to live in apartments as they provide additional features like shared maintenance and enhanced security at a lower cost.

199.   Should buildings be attractive to look at?

Although it can be a matter of personal choice however an attractive building is always better, not only to look at, it also gives a positive feeling to be living in or working out of a building that is attractive to look at has a lot of natural light, it can reduce the electricity cost with natural light available through the day. An attractive building may also attract a better price.

200.   Could you tell me about the area you are living in now?

I would recommend the readers to describe the area they are currently living in. while describing the area try to describe the positives of the area you may also highlight one or two shortcomings that you see in your area.

201.   Would you say your home town was a good place to bring up children? Why? Why not?

My home town is a small town and we had a great childhood, now when I have grown up I and see the difference between a mega city and a small town I realize it was a very good place to bring up children, there was no pollution in our town, we had some very good schools around, there were large grounds and open spaces for children to take up field sports, since it was a small town people knew each other well and there was great sense of community living and mutual caring.

202.   How easy is it in your city to meet new people?

As my city has lots of employment opportunities with multinational companies and a large number of people migrate to this city looking for job and business opportunities, it is very easy to meet new people, people from all walks of life come to this city and take up job or business.

203.   How do you feel about meeting people online?

Internet has made the world a true global village, one can meet and connect with any person across the world and sometimes it is a wonderful feeling to meet people online, learn different cultures and make friends with people who actually are complete strangers, However like any other platform online meeting also have to have a word of caution, I personally feel its okay to meet people online however ………………………

Practice Questions

204.	Could you tell me about the place where you were born?

205.	How have buildings in your hometown changed in last 10 years?

206.	Tell me about the main industries in your city.

207.	Where is your hometown?

208.	What are the main tourist attractions in your city/town?

Tourism:

209. What areas of a town or city do tourists often like to visit?

Tourists would often like to visit the part of city which has historical significance like, Forts and palaces; they may also like to visit a lake or any other place that is of tourist attraction. Some tourists like to visit street markets looking for handicrafts or unique items that they can carry home as memories.

210. How important is it for local Government to look after popular tourist attractions?

Any popular tourist attraction brings a large number of tourists to the place, in fact if you look at heritage cities around the world you would realize that these places get a huge number of tourists from different parts of the world, some may take it as study tour while for other it could be a part of their vacation, some may want their children to know and understand history. These tourists generate a lot of revenue for the city as they use other facilities like, Hotels, taxi services, restaurants, tour guide, purchasing mementos etc. Tourists help in creating a lot of employment opportunities for residents of the city, help in overall economy and generate additional tax revenue for the authorities. In my opinion it is imperative that local government looks after popular tourist attractions.

211.   Should people pay to visit attractions such as museums and galleries?

Museums and galleries have a fixed cost as well as a variable cost that the museum or gallery have to bear, many a times these places receive donations from government organizations, however they are providing service to society as they help in keeping the art, culture and history alive. I am of strong opinion that there should be a small amount of fee that is paid to visit these places that may help the museums and galleries cover a part of their cost as well as use the money for adding more of art and history to their existing list.

212.   How should tourists behave when they are in a different country?

Most of the countries now a days have tourist help centers with trained employees to guide tourists also most of the countries do publish a guideline for tourists so that tourists are aware of local culture and are sensitive to local beliefs. Tourist should keep themselves aware of these updates and in my opinion should remain as they are, they should enjoy the trip get as much learning as they can from their trip while keeping local traditions in mind.

213.   What can local people do to help tourists enjoy their visit?

Tourism is a big source of revenue generation for any society and country, It's the local people who benefit the most from tourism and increase in number of tourists is directly proportionate to income of local population, In my opinion local people should be friendly to tourist, understand the challenges the tourists may face and suggest the best options, even a simple help like sharing direction or suggesting a food outlet in a polite manner goes a long way in making the tourist feel good about the place and they become brand ambassadors for the place.

214.   What can tourists learn from visiting new places?

Since ancient time people have been travelling to new places to in search of knowledge, even in today's world tourism is a huge business as tourists go from one place to other, the purpose of visit may be different for different people, however knowledge about a new place, new culture, history of a place, primary business, lifestyle of local people , ancient architecture etc are a few things that tourists can learn about from visiting new places.

Practice Questions

215.   What are the benefits of visiting different countries?

216.   Are there any negative effects of tourism?

217.   What do you need to do before you go abroad on holiday?

218.   What type of problems can people have on holiday?

219.   How should countries encourage tourists to come to their country?

220.   How easy or difficult is it to travel around your country?

221.   What role does tourism play in your country's economy?

222.   Is there anything you don't like doing on holiday?

223.   Do you prefer to spend your holidays alone or with your family and friends?

224.   What is your favorite holiday activity?

225.   Do you enjoy traveling?

226.   Tell me about the best place you have ever visited

227.   Tell me about a country you especially like to visit? Why?

228.   What are the main tourist attractions there?

Newspapers:

229. When do people like to read the newspaper?

Most of the people like to read newspaper early in the morning, in face older generation had a habit of reading newspaper along with their breakfast, the habit still continues with most of the people, there is one noticeable change that is Internet newspaper, a lot of people specially younger generation like to read newspaper on an electronic device as they can scan through the news faster and also read it on the go.

230. How important is it for people to have a choice of newspaper?

Although in my opinion almost all newspapers cater to the same news, however some newspapers are more detailed and some may cover specific areas like Political News, Business and Economy or Sports more, this gives reader an option to choose from a list of newspapers as per their preference.

231. What does a good newspaper contain?

A good newspaper is one that provides News based on facts, publishes unbiased opinion, a newspaper has a wide range of readers and the newspaper should cater to the need of most sections of the society, someone may be interested in Political news, while other may be looking for something else like business news, sports, celebrity news. To summarize I think the newspaper must publish encouraging and positive thoughts.

232. Why do some people prefer to read the news on the internet rather than in newspaper?

Life is moving in fast lane these days and not everyone has time to read a physical newspaper, furthermore a lot of people may not be interested in all news, some people prefer to read news on the go, or at different times of the day, may be at work or during lunch break, Its easier for them to carry an electronic device like cell phone, I Pad etc. and read news at a time when they are free. Furthermore newspaper generally gets published at midnight and circulated in morning however the electronic newspaper can be updated with news throughout the day and presents latest news.

233.   How is internet news different from the news you read in the newspaper?

Basically the news is same however the fundamental difference between news paper and internet news is, Internet news can be updated every minute and we all want to have latest update.

234.   Will internet news ever replace newspaper? Why? Why not?

It may take time however it seems inevitable to me that one day internet news would overtake the newspaper, we are already aware that in some parts of western world smaller newspapers are closing and shifting to only online or internet news, as easy access to internet and convenience of reading newspaper on electronic device with most current updates is encouraging people to switch to internet news from traditional newspaper.

Animals:

235.   Many wild animals are rapidly becoming endangered or extinct. What are your views on this?

In the 18th and 19th century due to lack of awareness people would kill a lot of wild animals for fun or to display bravery, this led a lot of species to be endangered, however a lot of effort has been shown to protect the animals in last 50 years and it is showing a positive result, Now there is a new threat that is rising population of mankind, with rising population humans are encroaching on forest land for living and other resources like food, some of the species of animals and birds are getting endangered and this may create a threat to ecosystem, it must be taken as a collective responsibility by all to ensure we protect wildlife and save animals from being extinct

236.   In some countries people who own pets have to pay an annual fee. Do you think it should be a lot of money?

Having a dog as pet may seem to be a fun activity, however in reality dogs become a part of our lives, especially children get very attached to dogs, These days keeping a dog as pet is already a costly affair, with fixed expenses like visits to veterinary doctor on regular interval, having a health insurance for dogs, purchasing dog food etc. In my opinion the license fee must be kept at a minimum so that more people are encouraged to keep dogs as pets and don't leave them a street dogs.

237.   What might having a pet teach children?

Having a pet at home is like adding one more family member, they often act as stress busters to all, children get very attached with pets and love to play with them, having a pet at home teaches a child to be compassionate, caring and loving. Furthermore a pet may make a child more social than being a lonely person, even if adults in the house go to work the child feels they have the dog with them to play with or taking the dog out for a walk keeps the child busy and they don't feel lonely.

Sports:

238.   Have you ever played a team sport? What was it like?

Yes while I was in school and college, I played soccer and cricket and was part of my school team for both the games, it was a great learning experience for me to be a part of a team sport, I learnt how to be a better team member, how to coordinate with other team members, how does a captain or coach of the team communicate to the team and gets the team to work together towards a common goal. If I may say that I got my first lessons on being a team player, managing a team, coordinating and effective communication from this sport.

239.   Do you think men or women enjoy individual sport more? Why?

I don't think enjoying a sport is related to being a man or woman, in my opinion it is based on individual likings, skill sets and preferences. We all know men and women who enjoy individual sports more than team sports and also there are both men and women who enjoy team sports more than individual sports.

240.   Many people no longer watch sport as they think it has become too commercial. What is your opinion?

In my opinion a sport is a sport and there is not much change if the sport becomes commercialized, in fact with changing time the games that are shown live on television are mostly played in evenings so that more people can watch it, this in turn generates more revenue for sports administration and they can use it for further advancement of sports facilities and train new sportspersons.

241.   What skills do children learn from playing team sports?

Team sports are an excellent source of learning for children, children learn the art of sharing, caring, how to be a good team member, they learn the fact that a collective effort is always better than single efforts, some children learn leadership skills, managing a team helps them develop managerial skills, children also learn to be disciplined as they have to follow the team's collective goal not individual goals.

242.   Do you think it is possible these days not to be competitive?

In my opinion it would be extremely difficult for a person not to be competitive in today's world.
Today the world is moving in a fast pace there is always a race among all to be the best, there are always a technical or scientific invention that is being done, new technologies are making old technology obsolete, so in order to be a part of success story of today's society one must be competitive and has to always learn and evolve.

PART 2 Que Card Questions

1. Describe a useful website you have visited.

   You should say:

   what the website was

   how you found the address for this website

   what the website contained

   and explain why it was useful to you.

In today's tech savvy world everyone uses multiple websites every day, sometimes we may not even realize how much we as a society depend on websites for any and every thing we need, be it shopping, communication, business or education.

One website that I frequently visit and depend a lot for my needs is Google.

Google happens to be a search engine that can redirect one to a more specified website for an information, or it may have the information available itself, I was first introduced to Google almost 15 years back by one of my colleagues.

The website has been extremely useful for me, I use it for almost every search whether I am looking for directions or trying to know about a recent research, looking for updates about money market or simple searching some sports information.

2. **Talk about a book that you remember well.**

   You should say:

   What the title is and who wrote it

   What the books is about

   Why you read it

   And explain why you remember it well

I am inclined towards reading books since my school days and whenever I get time I try to read a new book, very recently I bought a book by the name of " Who moved my cheese" this book has been written by Dr Spencer Johnson.

This book is a an excellent book for looking for new frontiers in life and career.

The story is about two rats who live in an abandoned house that has tons of food supply for the rats and they have a great time, eating and relaxing is the only thing that the rats do.

After some time one of the rats decides to look around for other sources of food, however the other rat dismisses the idea of looking around and simple prefers to eat and sleep.

One of the rats goes around and finds some other sources of foods and comes back to share the news with his friend, his friend refuses to move out and continues to stay in the house.

The first rat goes to the new source of food and after few days decides to go back and look for his friend once he reaches the abandoned house he realized that his friend had not eaten for days and was extremely weak as one day the owners of the house came and moved all the food from the house and the rat had no place to go to search for new food he was left with no choice but to wait for house owners to come back with some food, Around the same time his friend had another source of food, finally both the rats move to the new place.

The story tells us that no matter how good the current situation is we must keep our eyes and ears open to see what is happening around. This will help us remain prepared for any untoward situation that may come around.

3. **Talk about a magazine or newspaper article that you read.**

    You should say

    When and where you read it

    What the article was about

    Why you read it

    And explain if you enjoyed it or not.

Recently I read an article about health care system in India and was pleasantly surprised to see a wonderful plan being initiated by the government. It was printed by almost all leading periodicals in India and around the world.

The Article was planned to give health insurance to a large population of India who can not afford to get quality medical treatment. As per the article the government is launching a new health care program for people below certain level of income and the insurance premium will be paid by the Government.

This will give a health insurance to those covered for a sum of half a million and would cover the entire family of the covered person, it will also reduce a lot of pressure from government health centers and will generate a large amount of business in private sector health care centers and will also generate a lot of employment opportunities in private health care system.

As I read through the article I was pleasantly surprised as a large number of people for low income group will have access to advanced health care facility and also create opportunities for young people to get employment in this sector.

4. **Talk about a television channel that you like.**

    You should say

    What the name of the channel is

    What types of programs it offers

    When you usually watch this channel

And explain why you like this channel.

Although I do not get enough time to watch television due to my difficult work schedule, however some times I do watch television to get some entertainment or information.

I generally like to watch History Channel as I find programs from this channel to be informative and mostly the programs are one hour in length and every episode completes in one hour. That is I don't need to wait for next episode to get complete information about the program.

I usually watch the shows on weekend, my preference of programs are those which are based on scientific research, space research and social issues from around the world.

Why I like the channel is because it give a fresh program every time and each of the program is informative, it gives some new information and knowledge every time I watch it.

5. **Talk about a job that you think is hard to do.**

    You should say:

    What it is

    Who usually does this job

    Where you learned about this job

    And explain why you think it is a hard job to do.

I am of the opinion that all jobs are difficult till we learn how to do it and till the time we do not love our respective jobs, some may think that a job in an office sitting in environment which is temperature controlled has fixed hours to reach office and leave office is an easy job but it may not be the case always.

In my opinion the job that is toughest is the job of security personnel be it civil police or military. While most of us have fixed working hours and mostly a defined work, in today's world security people may face a new challenge every day, they have to be on alert every given minute and are constantly on the lookout for unwanted elements from the society for the safety and security of common population of the society.

Whenever there is a festival or some kind of celebration the entire society meets with their friends and family and celebrate while security personnel are on alert to ensure safety of others.

Similarly military personnel are posted in most difficult terrain, sometimes they may be posted in hot desserts or extremely cold climate and while they are there they have to be on alert and one mistake can be fatal not only for one but for the entire team.

These are the reasons I feel these jobs are extremely difficult.

6. **Talk about a time that you helped someone.**

    You should say:

    Who you helped

    When you helped them

    What you helped them with

    And explain if it was difficult to help this person.

    It happened with me while I was working for a corporate company in USA, one of the employees working in my team was about to be lose his job due to low performance and the management had almost made up their opinion.

    The employee walked up to me and said she is scared of losing the job and also informed how badly she needed the job. She basically was requesting me to try and save her job.

    I could feel that she was willing to put in better efforts to improve her performance, I spoke to the human resources team and suggested we give this employee some more time, while the management had their own reasons to believe that the employee has been given enough time, I took it upon myself and suggested that I wish to work on her skills for next 90 days and that should improve her performance.

The management agreed and I took it upon myself to re train the employee and things changed, The employee showed tremendous improvement and went on to become one of the most successful employees.

I don't think it was difficult to train the employee, its just that she did not understand the basic concept of the work assigned to her, once she learnt it, the job became easier.

7. **Describe a sport or physical activity you did as a child.**

    You should say:

    Where you usually did the sport or activity

    How often you participated in it

    What it involved

    And also say if you like this sport or physical activity or not.

    During my school days I was very active with school sports team, my favorite game was soccer.

    We used to have practice session after school almost every day for two hours, during summer vacations we would practice in the morning hours.

    Practice used to be under watch of a coach or a senior player, it wuld involve physical exercise to warm up the body, taking rounds of the ground and then practicing on specific things like passes to players and on weekends we would have actual 90 minute practice matches.

    I was part of the team due to the fact that I had immense liking for the sport and even till date it enjoy this game, now I cant play as much however I am a member of soccer team for my organization.

8. **Talk about a sports event that you would like to attend.**

    You should say:

Where the event usually takes place

How often it occurs

Who you would like to attend with

And also explain why you would like to attend this sports event.

I used to be an active participant in sports during my school days and as the time passed by other commitments kept me out of professional sports, as of now I am an active player in corporate team tournaments that are organized once a year and I still participate in the practice sessions every weekend and watch sports on TV as and when I get time.

I have a long cherished dream to watch the world cup cricket final in a stadium, my desire is to be in stadium with friends and family to watch the game and have shared this with my friends, some of my friends have agreed to the plan.

This summer that is 2019 March/April cricket world cup is getting organized in Australia and the finals will be played in Sydney, We have planned to go on a vacation to Australia around that time and watch the final match. Hopefully this time I will be able to fulfill my desire, as it will be an event worth watching furthermore I will be able to live the excitement and fun of sitting in a big stadium to watch a great match.

9. **Describe a device that you often use.**

   You should say:

   What the device is and what it looks like

   How you got it

   What you use it for

   And explain if you like this device or not.

One devise that I use most often is my cell phone, this is an I phone 7 which was gifted to me by my wife.

The phone brings in a large number of features and is easy to use, In a way, I am almost dependent on the phone for almost all official needs and also use it for personal purposes.

Of course it's a phone and I use it to connect with my collegues, family and friends via phone calls or messaging services like whattsapp, messanger etc.

Other uses are email, mobile banking, getting driving directions, scanning of documents, or even ordering food the phone is useful for all purposes.

I use it extensively and for sure I like it for all the features it has to offer.

10. Describe an important letter/email that you sent to someone.

You should say:

When you sent the letter/email

Who you sent the letter/email to

What the purpose of the letter/email was

And explain if this was a difficult letter/email to write.

Every year in the month of January my company announces promotions of employees and most employees look forward to it as they have their own aspirations or goals.

As I am working as Manager of a large team and my team has been successfully working and achieving goals month after month, in the month of January I was expecting a promotion for myself and also for some of my team members.

However as per the report received from human resources team no one from my team was promoted including me, it was disheartening I could possibly accept but how about team members, they definitely will be upset may be we end up losing some extremely talented personnel. These thoughts made me upset and I decided to write a mail to my senior vice president about it. I wanted him to realize that I am not convinced with their thoughts about zero promotions from a team which was getting excellent results.

While I was drafting the mail, I was making too many self corrections as I wanted to raise a question however did not want to sound rude or impulsive. I took out my team's performance data for the year and attached with the mail.

To my surprise the leadership team took notice of my mail and agreed to go for a reevaluation.

11. Describe something you do to keep healthy.

You should say:

What the activity is

When you do it

How often you do it

And explain why you think it is a good way to look after your health.

In recent years I have noticed a great amount of awareness has been created by different organizations about being health conscious, there are various scientific reports out in public domain that talk about activities we must do keep ourselves healthy. These reports also share age wise need of health activities and how dining habits impact our health.

In order to remain healthy and fit, I take a walk everyday in te evening after my work, there is a park close to my society where I go in the evening and take a walk, one complete walking trail is of 2 kilometers and I generally take two rounds of the trail.

It helps my body release a lot of stress, gives me happiness and satisfaction that I am taking care of my body, furthermore it helps me get a good sleep. Apart from this I try to participate in some kind of sporting activity over the weekend, sometimes I play table tennis and occasionally I also play badminton.

12. **Describe a time when you were ill.**

You should say:

When this was

What your symptoms were

How long the illness lasted

And say how it affected your life at the time.

All of us want to remain healthy and enjoy each day of our lives and many a times we don't care about our own body and this makes us sick sometimes.

This is what happened to me in March this year we were going for annual closing in the office and had a lot of workload, I basically got so involved with my work that I did not realize the work was taking a toll on my body.

By the time we completed our annual closing I was down with fever and the doctor suggested a complete bed rest for 7 days. I would feel week and tired throughout the day food did not taste well at all and on top of that there were medicines that tasted awfully bad to say the least.

It was an extremely boring 7 days of my life, where in I was away from my work and not that I was on vacation, I was sick simple lying in the bed with nothing to do. Thankfully it did not last long and I was back to my regular life the next week.

13. **Describe somewhere you like to shop for food.**

You should say:

Where this place is

What this place is like

What you buy there

and explain why you like buying food at this place.

Shopping that too shopping for grocery in not something that I enjoy at all, for me it's a work that should be completed in short time. This is the reason I prefer to shop at a departmental store which has all items stacked at designated place and makes it easier and faster to shop.

I prefer to shop at a store by the name of "Mad Bananas" it is located in a shopping mall very close to the area we live in. It's a large store and has a large number of varieties available to choose from, they hallways maintain a good stock of fresh and frozen vegetables, almost all grocery items that we require for our day to day needs.

They also have an international section to buy international food items and the most interesting part is they have a section for snacks like sandwiches, burgers etc that are freshly made as per order.

These are the reasons I like this store it caters to almost all our grocery/food needs, its convenient and not very crowded and being a privileged member we also get a decent discount on products here.

14. Describe a meal that you enjoyed eating in a restaurant.

You should say:

Where the restaurant was

What you ate

Who ate the meal with you

and explain why you enjoyed eating the meal so much.

I am by nature a foodie and luckily my wife is fond of trying new food items as well, we have a set of our favorite restaurants where we visit during weekend and try different cuisines.

Only last weekend me and my wife visited an Italian restaurant for lunch and it was not very crowded, we asked the server to suggest something new and he recommended we try their vegetarian pastas with different sauces like tomato white or spinach, he recommended one more delicacy that is meat balls in mozzarella sauce.

We ordered the meal and it was excellent, it tasted very fresh was prepared as per our choice and was served piping hot. After a long time we were having such an excellent food and also the service personnel were very caring, this entire experience was enjoyable.

15. Describe an interesting journey you have been on.

You should say:

Where you went

How you travelled

Who you went with

and say how the journey affected your life.

In the year 2018 during summer vacations of our children we decided to visit Himachal, a state in the Himalayas as we wanted to explore life in smaller towns and villages in the Himalayas, we started on a weekend in my car and it took us six hours to reach our first destination chamba a small town that is not very famous with tourists, we stayed in a small hotel and for next three days with help of local guides, we travelled to few small towns nearby and also spent time in countryside.

It was overall a great experience on one hand we could see great views of Himalayas, farms in the area, grazing cows and sheep. On the other hand we got to know a lot about lifestyle of people living in the area, their joys their struggle etc.

The journey definitely made impact on our lives we could understand that people out there had a much more peaceful and easy life as compared to us, we always thought that city life is better but after this trip we realized that these people may not have a lot of money but they certainly get to enjoy their life more than us.

16. Describe an important industrial unit in your country

You should say:
What the industrial unit is
How you know it
Why it is important
And explain how much you like the unit.

I recently got a chance to visit a Cell phone manufacturing plant in my country, actually I was part of a team that was sent to study a manufacturing plant as part of my course.

We visited a plant for Samsung mobile phones, it is one of the largest mobile phone plant for Samsung worldwide, the plant was operational for last couple of years but recently the company had decided to increase the capacity of the plant by three times as they would use this plant to cater to not only the domestic market but also exports.

This was all over the news as it was inaugurated by chairman of Samsung worldwide and Prime Minister of India, this plant is already providing jobs to more than ten thousand employees and almost five thousand external vendors, that is a lot of employment generated for the country and a major source of income for country in terms of taxes.

We were taken to different sections of the plant like assembling section, headsets etc. I liked the plant as it was very well planned, a lot of latest technology was used to built the plan and the sheer volume of cellular phones that it produces every day.

17. **Describe a city that you have visited.**
    where the city is (and its name)
    when you went there
    what you liked / disliked about the city
    and explain why you visited this city.

I Recently went to Mumbai for a business trip, I had to attend three different meetings in a span of two days, the meetings were each of thirty minutes and since it was an official trip I was fully prepared for the meetings that ways I had a lot of time to myself, on day one I could complete both my meetings by 11.30 in the morning and next meeting was scheduled for next afternoon.

I decide to take a tour of city, visited different areas like, Chowpatty beach, Nariman point, crawford market and decided to have snacks at different famous places.
I found the city to be crowded, be it market place or a tourist attraction or even a hotel however the city was full of life there was not a dull moment in the city, be it restaurants, clubs or beach, everywhere I found the city to be in running in fast pace lots of small and large businesses offering great service at reasonable rates.

Overall I like the city for its fast paced life, tons of commercial activities and openness in the people towards visitors.

18.   Describe a leisure activity near or on the sea
   You should say:
   What it is
   Who do you play with
   Why you have to prepare
   And explain how you feel about it

I basically live far away from Sea so do not get chance to do a lot of sporting activity around the sea.
However last summer vacation I took my family to a Goa and the intention was to enjoy the sandy beaches. Myself and my wife decided to play with our children on the beach, we did some preparation for the game, like getting a football and some other light colorful balls from the hotel desk.

We started with soccer and ended up playing multiple games like kicking the ball in air, sometimes towards the sea, sometimes against the sea with the wind.

It was a wonderful morning of sporting activities for almost four hours followed by a wonderful breakfast, light swimming at the sea and lazing around at the beach.

This truly was a wonderful experience for the entire family.

19.   Describe an organization or company where you live and they employs a lot of people.
   You should say:
   What it is
   How many employees work there
   What its work
   And explain what you think about it.

I am inclined to live this one to students to decide which company they want to talk about.

I recommend you to speak about your current employer or a company where you intend to work.

You may obtain data from their website as well, # of employees, annual revenue, major services or products offered, employee policies.

Most importantly I suggest a positive feedback about the company, no need to describe the company in negative tone.

20. Describe a happy event from your childhood that you remember well.
You should say:
What the event was
When and where it happened
What you saw or did
And explain why you remember this event so well

During my school days after the mid term examinations our school used to organize different competition in sports and arts as well as completions like debate, essay writing etc.

I was good in sports and would participate in athletic events and would win some prizes every year in my category. It was when I was in 8th grade my class teacher suggested that I should participate in essay as well as debate competition, he was keen to guide me for these competitions.

I followed his instructions and prepared hard for both essay as well as debate competition.

The results were to be announced on the annual day celebration of our school, My parents were present in the program as well and I knew I would be getting some awards for sports events but was not sure if I would win any other competition, when the results were announced for Debate and Essay competition, I had won the debate competition and got a special mention for my essay writing.

It was truly a memorable event for me as my teachers were happy as well as parents, who did not expect me to win in different categories, even I was pleasantly surprised.

20. Describe a person who solved a problem in a clever way
who the person is
when you meet the person
where do you
and explain why do you think the person is clever

I work for a corporate company where in we undertake projects from our clients and once the project is completed we implement on client site, sometimes it takes more efforts to implement the project than creating the project itself, I remember one such incident we had completed the project and in our testing it was fully functional but when we tried to implement it would fail at client site, we tried couple of times and it was not working at all.

Finally we decided to call in an expert form a different section in the same office, this is the first time when I met this person, he was a veteran of implementation and had been working for last 20 years in implementation.

This person sat with us in a meeting, looked at all aspects of project and asked the client team to come on line and share their updates on how the implementation was falling on their end, what messages they were getting. The client team shared their updates and our expert asked if they have added any new software to their existing set up to which they replies affirmative, and that was the cause client changed their software system without informing us and that is the reason the project was not getting up loaded.

21. Describe a statue or art.

You should say:
What it looks like
Where you saw it
Did you like it
And why you think it is special.

I have seen many statues around in life, generally the statues are made in honor of great contributors to the society or country, But one such statue that I would like to talk about is statue of unity, It is the tallest statue in the world and was recently inaugurated by prime minister of the country.

In the month of Oct 2018 it was in news all around the country that the tallest statue of world is ready to be inaugurated and would be available for visitors to see, I also decided to take a tour over the weekend to see the statue and get more information about it.

It's a huge statue of Sardar patel the first home minister of India also known as Iron man of India, its completely made of brass and is situated on the banks of Narmada river, one can get a ticket to get an up close view of the statue, in face it can be seen from a long distance as well, the statue has an elevator which takes viewers to a height and offers a wonderful view of blue waters on Narmada river and it valley, there are lots of historical information placed on the walls that tells us about the life and work of Sardar patel and his contribution towards the country.

In my opinion it is a special tribute to the great Leader and at the same time it will get the younger generation to know more about the Sardar Patel.

22. **Describe a bicycle tour.**
You should say:
When you had this trip
Who went on with you
What did you do during this trip
And explain why you like it.

I am member of bicycle trekking team, the team generally meets every Sunday morning and goes for a bicycle trek in the aravali hills forest area, there is a large cycling trec that has been made and at some places the trek is broken that is we have to ride on ground which could be dusty or muddy.

Recently I and two of my friend decided to take a Trek away from our group and get into other zones of the thick forest and hilly terrain. It was extremely exciting as at some places we had to carry our bicycle in hand and again ride it. The hills were presenting a great view with green cover all around, we were able to notice different birds and animals like monkeys and wild cats, at one place we also noticed rabbits.

We were surprised as to so close to a City which is more of a concrete jungle there was so much that nature was offering us, we noticed so many natural water bodies like ponds etc. and I must say this day was one of the best days that I spent on Bicycle in a green area.

23.   Describe an enjoyable day spent in the countryside
You should say:
When and where you went
Who you went with
What you did there
And explain why you think it was enjoyable

In the beginning of Nov this year Me and my friend decided to go for a small vacation in the hills and we started for a town in hills, since it was a holiday we did not encounter much traffic and by 10 am we were at a distance of 15 kilometers from our destination, we decided to have a breakfast in a countryside eatery.

While having breakfast and sipping tea we realized it was a wonderful setting in the country side, we were looking at hills, farms some mango grooves in the distance, we decided to walk down the village and spend some time there, it was a great experience to have breakfast in the fields with cows grazing around, goats and other farm animals.

We had stopped there for having breakfast but decided to spend next four five hours talking to local people, roaming around the streets of the village, enjoying its natural settings and finally we tried local delicacies for lunch before leaving for our next destination.

24. Describe a decision made by that you disagree with
You should say:

Who made this decision
What it is
How you told him/her
And explain why you disagree the decision

I have worked in corporate sector in managerial capacity for a long period and by the nature of my job, many a times we have to take a collective decision and not always my opinion would be collective decision that is on multiple occasions I had to agree with other's opinion even if my decision would be a different one.

I would like to mention one such incident where in I was of opinion that we as a company must outsource part of our work to a more specialized vendor and that would make our job easier, faster and even the quality of work would be good as the vendor has employees with more experience in the field. However my proposal received a pushback from senior leadership team as they wanted us to develop a team for the same.

I spoke to my Vice President and explained my thoughts however he suggested that the long term goal of company was to create our own team of specialized personnel with requisite skills even if it means some losses now but can yield great results in future.

25. **Describe an interesting house or an apartment you visited.**
You should say:
Where it was
Whose home it was
What it looks like
And explain why you think it was interesting?

This year in the month of may I went to United states with my group as we were transitioning a project from United states to India, while this was a fully occupied trip with lots of work, meetings, trainings etc. Somehow me and my counterpart developed a good bonding and on weekends when I would be majorly free. My friend invited me to see his farm house which was almost 15 miles from our workplace.

We started one early morning with my friend and his wife picking me up from my hotel, they drove me to this farm house which was not huge but was in a peaceful countryside setting, while on the farm house I realized they had taken a great effort in creating a unique house, it was a small house but had features like large balcony, sun room and a yard, they did not have any domestic animal but there were wild Geese, Rabbits and Deer in the area which would graze in their yard, The house was just good enough for a couple and a guest however had features like pool table, bar area, grill area, study room with plenty of sun light.

Overall it was a wonderful house, which offered breath taking views of countryside with hills in the background, there were lush green areas around and the house seemed to attract me because of the calmness that it offered with almost all major amenities in a small area.

26. Describe a kind of foreign food you tried.
   You should say:
   What it was
   When and where you had it
   Why you had it
   And explain how you felt it.

I am basically a foodie and love to try new kind of food every now and then, recently I was on an official trip to united states of America and was introduced to a new food product there that is Buffalo Wings.

This is a chicken delicacy that originated in town of Buffalo and thus got its name, these are wings of chicken which are marinated and deep fried and is served with a tangy sause.

I was taken to a restaurant in Buffalo by my colleagues in Buffalo during my last visit, the restaurant was extremely famous and in the past even president of USA had visited this place. I was little unsure as to how it would taste but as I had it I realized it was a great food item. Later I started having this almost every day till I was in Buffalo.

27.   Describe an interesting neighbor
   You should say:
   Who this person is
   How you know this person
   What this person like to do
   And explain why you think this neighbor is interesting

I am not much popular person in my neighborhood and basically have only few friends around my society, one person in my friends group from my society is Mr Sharma, he is quite an interesting character and is a wonderful neighbor to have.

Mr Sharma happens to be a software professional and works for a multinational company, I came in touch with him during one of the social gatherings in my society, He seems to have a lot of time that he devotes towards society meetings, group activities, organizing some sports and cultural activities for society members. Mr Sharma is always high in energy and commitment towards these causes and generally he is the announcer/presenter during most of these events.

He makes any event interesting by using his sense of humor and exciting way of presentation. These are the reasons I believe he is a very interesting person, very social, great sense of humor a wonderful organizer and overall a trustworthy person.

28.   Describe a shop that just opened in your hometown.
You should say:
Where the shop is
When it opened
What it sells
And how you feel about the shop?

Recently I received a promotional text message that said a new store of Big Bazaar is opening in my neighborhood and it was actually an invitation to join the opening ceremony along with some discount vouchers. This was a pleasant surprise as I am a frequent customer to this store brand which is a bit far from my place. I was excited as it would ease shopping for my family and we don't need to drive far.

The shop is located in a mall almost one kilometer from my house, it started its operation on Nov 1st 2018, it has all the features one may look from a departmental store, like groceries, clothing, upholstery, electronics, cosmetics, toys and even vegetables.

I love to sop at this store as they offer a wide range of products with plenty of verieties to choose from, the prices they have is reasonable and many a times is economical as compared to other shops, furthermore since I am a privilege club member for them I get additional discounts and cash backs along with loyalty points and these are the reasons why this is my favorite shopping place.

29. **Describe a future plan which is not related to work or study**
   What the plan is
   When you thought of the plan
   Who is involved in the plan
   and say how you think you will achieve the plan.

One of the most important future plans that I have is to make a retirement house, I was raised in a small town and for higher studies moved to a mega city, subsequently for employment also I have been staying in a large city. However I have a desire to build a retirement home close to beach in a peaceful area, I have already though about it and zeroed on couple of regions and planning to either buy a unit that is already existing or get a custom house constructed.

I thought of this idea some five years back and my wife is involved with me on this also our children are upbeat about this house.

My plan is to save some money for now and once my kids get in to college use the saved amount and may be top it up with a small loan and start the construction of the house, once we get on to it the work can be completed in 6 months or so, its just that we may take some more years to save up for this long pending thought.

30. Describe a kind of weather that you like

You should say:
What it is
What you usually do in this kind of weather
How you felt about it
And explain what influences it may bring to you

My favorite weather is Spring season, it generally comes in the month of February and March each year, that is after the long and cold winter season and just before the hot summer.

This season opens up the sporting time as the most of the sports tournaments are played around this time, it also gives a positive vibe with bright sunlight after gloomy winters and is not extremely hot like summers, what we notice is flowers bloom all around the society.

Generally I like to take out time for outdoor activities like playing soccer, taking a walk or simply soaking in the sun. some times I also like to take a long drive outside the city and just enjoy nature in the countryside.

This season actually brings a lot of positive thoughts, planning for the long summer and starting a new project that is the reason I like this season to be the best.

31.. **Describe an interesting talk or speech you heard recently.**
You should say:
Who was the person you talk to
Where and when you talked with this person
What you talked about with this person
And explain why it was interesting?

I am normally inclined to know about the success story of different personalities, recently I watched a talk show by one of the famous artists in Hindi film industry, his name is Pankaj Tripathy. I watched his interview on YouTube conducted by a famous channel.

Watching this talk I learnt that this successful actor actually came from a humble family and worked hard to get good education with simple means, He desired to be a successful actor which was a far cry for someone coming from his part of the country, but this individual was not willing to give up his dreams. He decided to enroll in to the best acting training school in the country and did odd jobs like selling shoes as a commission agent to different businesses. He also worked as chef in a hotel to support his education.

Finally he made into his desired acting school and started a lot of theater furthermore he decided to try his hand in film industry, where it was one step at a time for him, initially he was offered smaller roles that would give him survival money for him and his family, he continued to work on his own skills and over a period of time became a busy actor with lots of work at hand and later on he became an extremely successful actor.

The entire talk was extremely motivating and can inspire many to dream and work towards the success.

32. **Describe a famous person in your country.**
   You should say:
   Who this person is
   How you know this person
   What this person famous for
   And explain why you like this person.

There are many famous personalities in my country that I admire, but one person who I would rate extremely high is Ex president of India Dr A P J Kalam, Mr Kamal had a humble start to his life and studied at different schools before attending college to be a post graduate in science, further he was rejected for many jobs that he tried to get into, however he was determined and finally he became a nuclear scientist, Mr Kalam spearheaded the Nuclear research for India and successfully conducted nuclear tests that not only gave India an edge in defense but also proved vital for future energy needs of India.

I came to know about him while I was in college and we were taught about his life in college, there are many reasons I like or admire him just to mention here, he did not let his humble background stop him from thinking of what he wanted to achieve, he fought against all hardships to acquire knowledge and skills, initial failures did not deter him and he became more resilient in his approach towards his work.

He was a visionary and could foresee country's needs in future based on nuclear technology and achieved a great success for India.

Printed in Great Britain
by Amazon